THIS BOOK BELONGS TO

Love

Love

www.ingramcontent.com/pod-product-compliance
Lightning Source LLC
Chambersburg PA
CBHW081724220526
45468CB00008B/1970
* 9 7 8 1 9 8 4 1 1 7 6 4 9 *